Origami

Book One

Japanese paper-folding

by FLORENCE SAKADE

CHARLES E. TUTTLE COMPANY
Rutland, Vermont & Tokyo, Japan

Published by the Charles E. Tuttle Company, Inc.
of Rutland, Vermont & Tokyo, Japan
with editorial offices at
Suido 1-chome, 2–6, Bunkyo-ku, Tokyo, Japan

© *1957 by Charles E. Tuttle Co., Inc.*

Library of Congress Catalog Card No. 57–10685
International Standard Book No. 0–8048–0454–0

First edition, 1957
Eighty printing ,1997

PRINTED IN SINGAPORE

table of contents

Origami, the stimulating hobby of paper-folding, is a favorite pastime with Japanese children. Some of the extremely complicated designs that can be created with only a piece of paper and some nimble fingers are truly astonishing. For the beginner, I have chosen some of the simpler designs—those which, with practice and patience, can be learned by any-one who would like to master an art which has flourished in Japan for more than ten centuries.

The most difficult object in this book to make is the crane, but then, it is also the most fun, and once you have mastered it, it will be a real achievement. In Japan, the crane is a symbol of good luck and can be found, in some form or other, practically any place—even in some of the designs on women's kimonos. The folded-paper crane shown on the cover of this book is especially popular. Often, folded cranes of all sizes are strung on pieces of thread and hung from the ceiling to decorate the room. They also have a religious meaning, especially in country areas, where they are hung from the ceilings of shrines and temples as offerings from the people who go there to pray.

Generally, colored paper about four to six inches square is used. For a mixed-color effect, two sheets of different colors may be used by placing them back to back. After you reach a point where you consider your-self rather skillful, it would be interesting if you tried to make some-thing with a piece of paper only one inch square as Japanese children do to show their ability. For the present, however, I suggest that the following points be kept in mind:

A. All of the objects illustrated in the diagrams of this book are to be made from square pieces of paper. Five- or six-inch squares are the easiest to work with. Use thin paper, not heavy construction or art paper.

B. It is a good idea to practice making an object with ordinary paper so as not to waste colored paper.

C. If the directions seem to be complicated, you can mark the corners of the paper to correspond with the markings in the diagrams. The in-structions can be more easily followed in this way.

It is my hope, in writing this book, that the children of other coun-tries will find an interest in this creative pastime and, in making these charming little figures, will come to know the fun to be found in mak-ing things by themselves.

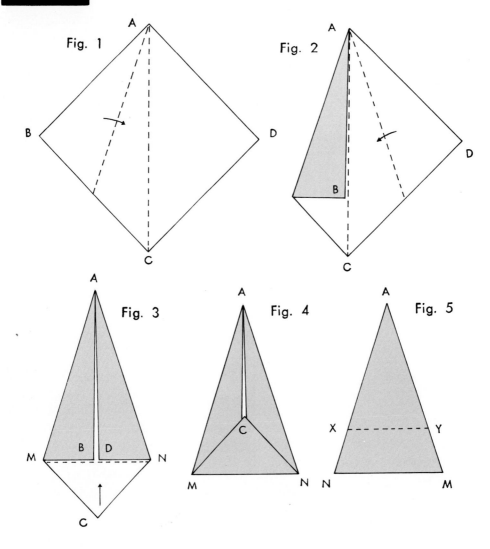

1. Fold a square piece of paper (Fig. 1) so that the edge AB extends over as far as the center line AC as shown in Fig. 2.
2. Do the same with AD in order to get Fig. 3.
3. Fold along MN so that point C is over and above points B and D. See Fig. 4.
4. Turn the paper over and fold back MN along XY (about two-fifths of the way up – Fig. 5) to get Fig. 6.

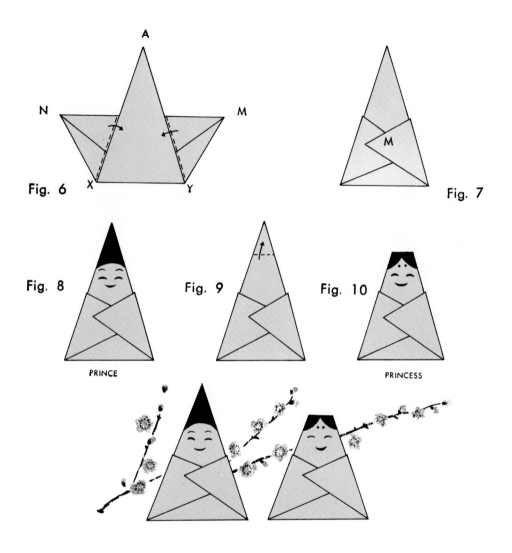

A

N   M

Fig. 6   X   Y

M

Fig. 7

Fig. 8

PRINCE

Fig. 9

Fig. 10

PRINCESS

5. Fold points M and N forward along AY and AX so as to overlap each other as in Fig. 7.
6. Complete doll by drawing face (Fig. 8).
7. To make a princess (Fig. 10), fold back the top of the head as shown in Fig. 9.

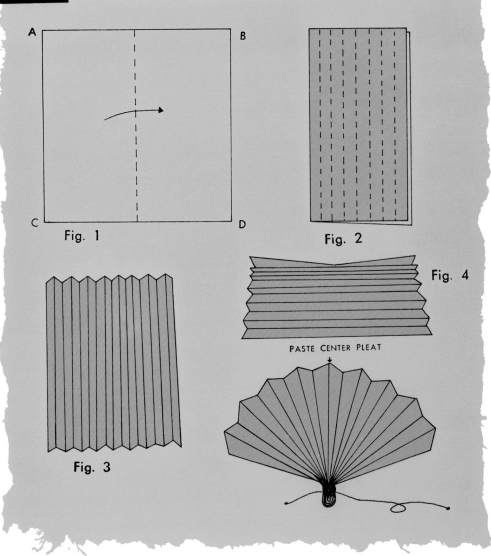

Fig. 1

Fig. 2

Fig. 4

Fig. 3

PASTE CENTER PLEAT

1. Take a square piece of paper and fold in half (Fig. 1). Make lengthwise folds (accordion fashion) across the entire breadth of the paper (Fig. 2) and then open to get Fig. 3.
2. Fold in half as shown in Fig. 4 and paste the center pleats together.
3. To complete, tie a piece of string about one-half an inch up from the bottom. See Fig. 5.

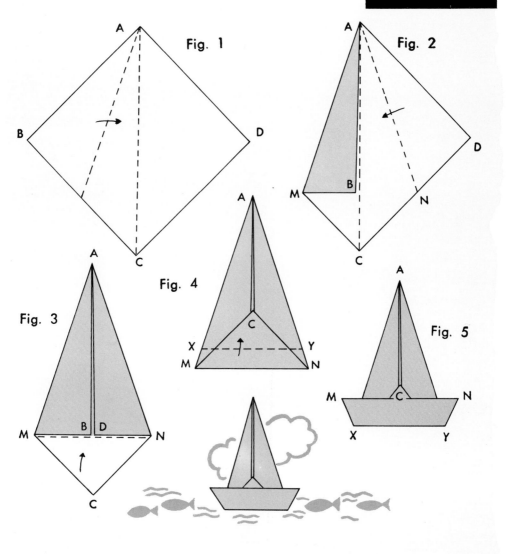

Fig. 1

Fig. 2

Fig. 3

Fig. 4

Fig. 5

1. Take a square piece of paper and fold it along line AC so that point B meets point D. Crease and then reopen as in Fig. 1.
2. Fold AB over to meet the center line AC (Fig. 2).
3. Do the same with AD so as to make Fig. 3.
4. Fold along line MN so that point C is above points B and D. See Fig. 4.
5. To complete, fold along line XY so that points M and N appear as in Fig. 5.

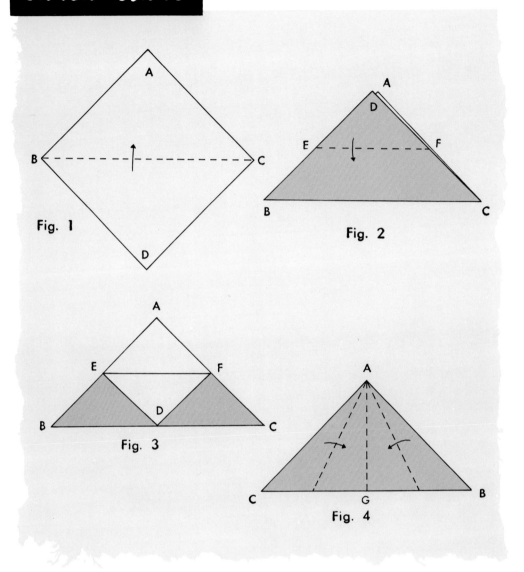

Fig. 1

Fig. 2

Fig. 3

Fig. 4

1. Fold a square piece of paper (Fig. 1) at BC so that point D is over point A, resulting in Fig. 2.
2. Fold at EF so that point D is brought forward to touch line BC at the center as shown in Fig. 3.
3. Turn the paper over as in Fig. 4. Bring AC forward until it is lined up on the center line AG. Do the same with AB and the result will be Fig. 5.

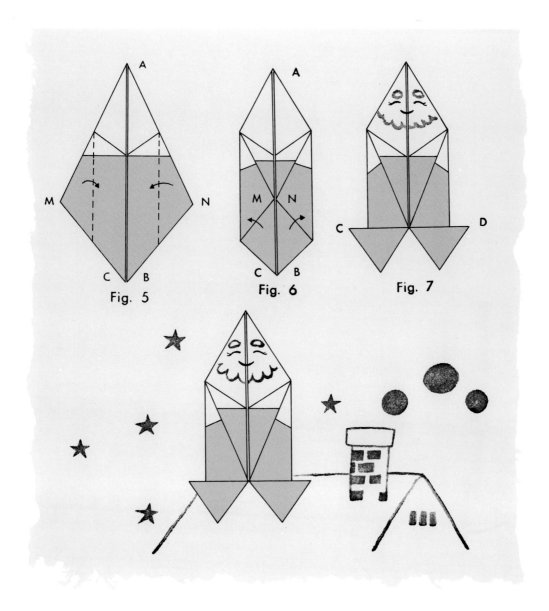

Fig. 5

Fig. 6

Fig. 7

4. Bring point M forward and fold on the dotted line shown in Fig. 5 so that M touches line AC. Do the same with point N and you will have Fig. 6.
5. Lift up point C and fold it over to the left as shown in Fig. 7. Do the same with point B, folding it over to the right.
6. To complete, draw in Santa's face.

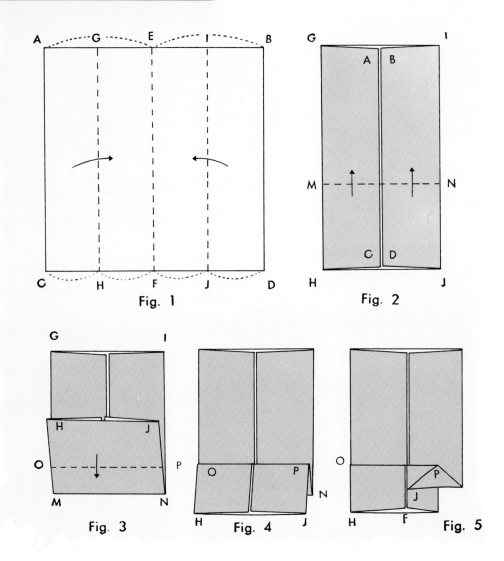

Fig. 1

Fig. 2

Fig. 3   Fig. 4   Fig. 5

1. Take a square piece of paper and fold it at GH and at IJ (Fig. 1) so that edges AC and BD meet at the center, EF, as in Fig. 2.
2. Fold at MN, about two-fifths of the way up, so that the edge HJ appears as in Fig. 3.
3. Fold at OP so that HJ appears as in Fig. 4.
4. Fold point J over to the left so that it is above F as shown in Fig. 5. Note that in doing so, point P is raised toward you and opened up

12

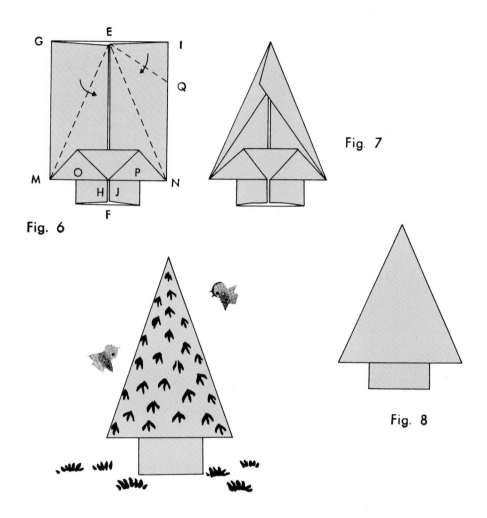

Fig. 6

Fig. 7

Fig. 8

so that it is in a new position and is no longer a corner. Do the same with H to get Fig. 6.

5. Fold along EM bringing point G forward.
6. Fold the corner I forward at EQ so it touches EN.
7. Fold along EN bringing point Q forward. The result is shown in Fig. 7.
8. Turn the paper over and draw Christmas tree decorations.

13

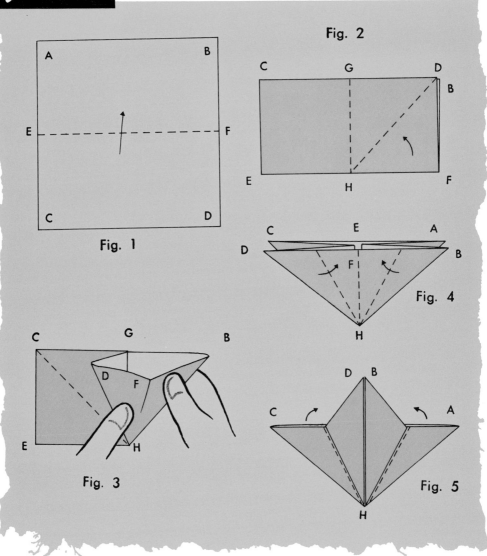

Fig. 1

Fig. 2

Fig. 3

Fig. 4

Fig. 5

1. Fold a square sheet of paper in the middle (Fig. 1) at EF in order to get Fig. 2.
2. Crease in the middle at GH and reopen.
3. Bring the corner F up between D and B so that it meets G, thus placing HF along GH. See Fig. 3. DHB will then form an upside-down triangle.
4. Repeat the step with E to get Fig. 4.

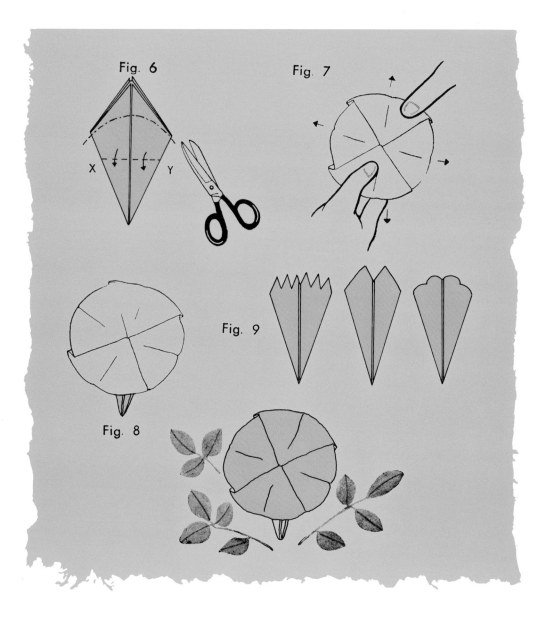

Fig. 6

Fig. 7

Fig. 9

Fig. 8

5. Bring the corners B and D forward to meet at the center over FH as in Fig. 5.
6. Turn the paper over and do the same with A and C.
7. Cut off the points with a pair of scissors as shown in Fig. 6.
8. Open the petals, as shown in Fig. 7, as far down as XY and you will get Fig. 8.
9. It is possible to make different kinds of flowers by cutting the petals into various shapes. See Fig. 9.

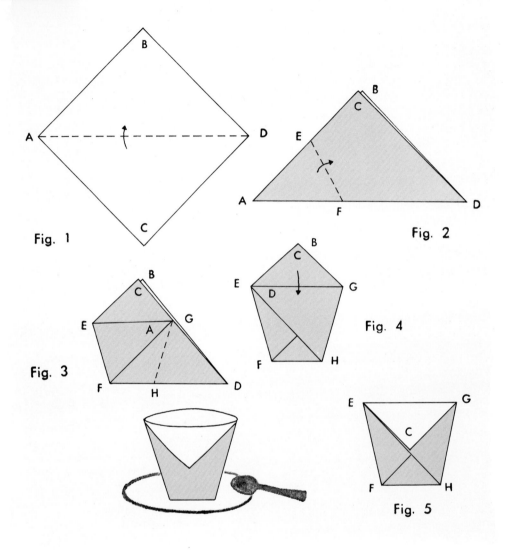

Fig. 1

Fig. 2

Fig. 3

Fig. 4

Fig. 5

1. Fold a square piece of paper along line AD (Fig. 1) so that point C is on top of point B as in Fig. 2.
2. Fold at EF so that point A extends over to the edge CD at point G, and so that EG is parallel to FD as in Fig. 3.
3. Do the same thing with point D so that DG is on top of EA as in Fig. 4.
4. Finish the cup by separating points C and B, folding point C forward along EG and folding point B in the opposite direction along EG. The finished cup is shown in Fig. 5.

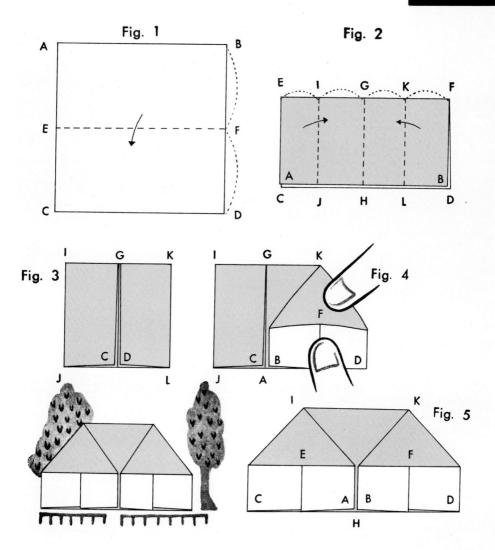

1. Fold a square piece of paper at EF (Fig. 1) so that edge AB is on top of edge CD as in Fig. 2.
2. Fold the edges AEC and BFD forward so that they meet at the center line GH as shown in Fig. 3.
3. Separate points B and D by holding B in place and swinging point D over to the right, thus bringing point F to the position shown in Fig. 4.
4. Do the same with points ECA (swinging C to the left) and you will have the paper house shown in Fig. 5.

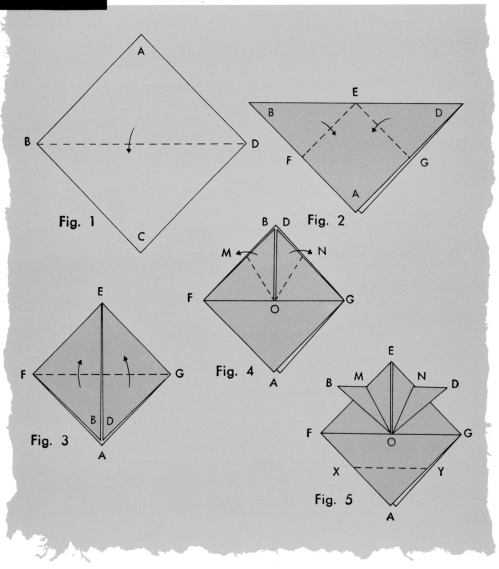

Fig. 1

Fig. 2

Fig. 3

Fig. 4

Fig. 5

1. Fold a square piece of paper along line BD (Fig. 1) so that corner A is over corner C as shown in Fig. 2.
2. Fold along EF and EG so that corners B and D meet at point A as in Fig. 3.
3. Fold up points B and D so that they meet at E as shown in Fig. 4.
4. Bring forward point B and fold this flap along OM as shown in Fig. 5. Point M is about one-third of the way down EF.

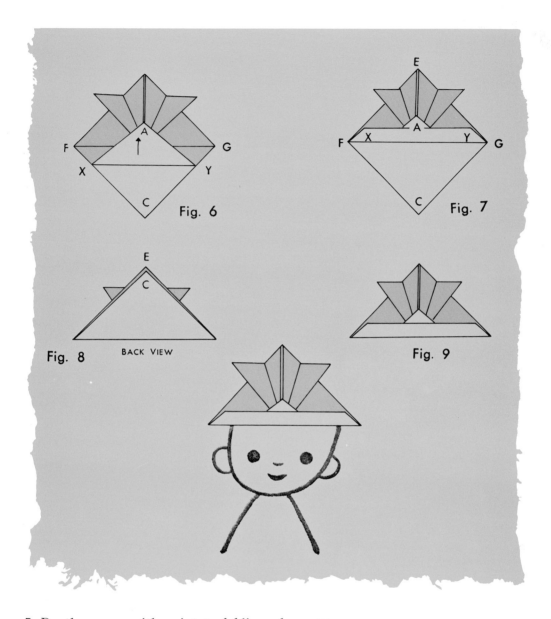

5. Do the same with point D, folding along ON.
6. Fold at XY (Fig. 6) so that point A is over and above point O.
7. Fold this front flap again at FG making Fig. 7.
8. Turn over and fold C so it meets E (Fig. 8).
9. Turn over again and you have Figure 9.

ship

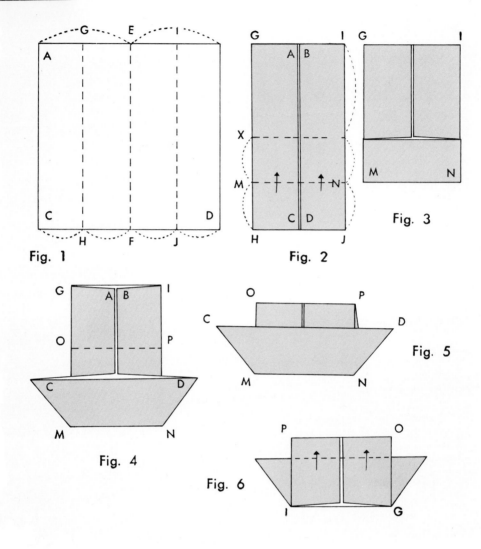

Fig. 1

Fig. 2

Fig. 3

Fig. 4

Fig. 5

Fig. 6

1. Fold a square piece of paper down the center on line EF as shown in Fig. 1, crease, and then unfold.
2. Fold at GH and IJ so that edges AC and BD meet at the center line EF. This results in Fig. 2.
3. Fold at MN so that edge HJ reaches the center line XY, thus forming Fig. 3.
4. Pull out corners C and D in order to form Fig. 4.
5. Fold backwards at OP so that the edge GI is directly under MN as shown in Fig. 5.

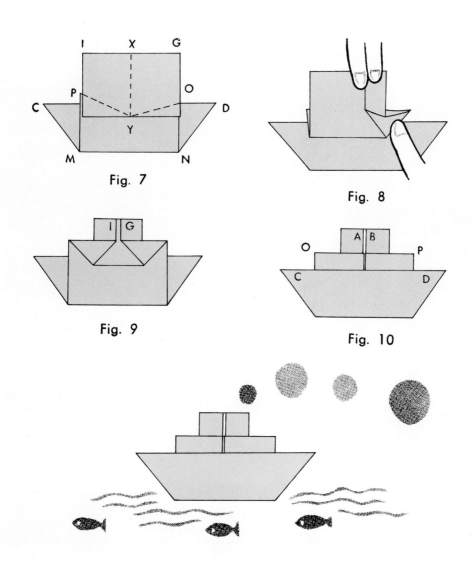

Fig. 7

Fig. 8

Fig. 9

Fig. 10

6. Turn over to get Fig. 6.
7. Fold so that the edge IG is over and above PO as in Fig. 7.
8. Bring point G forward and to the left so that it is directly over X, which is in the center. Fig. 8 shows how this is done. Do the same with point I in order to get Fig. 9.
9. Turn over and you have the ship shown in Fig. 10.

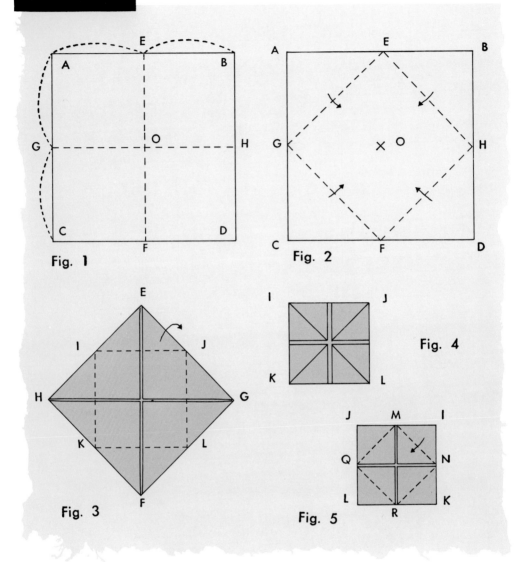

Fig. 1

Fig. 2

Fig. 3

Fig. 4

Fig. 5

1. Crease a square piece of paper as shown in Fig. 1 and then spread open.
2. Fold the four corners A, B, C and D forward so that they meet at the center as in Figs. 2 & 3.
3. Turn over and fold the four corners E, F, G and H so that they meet at the center as in Fig. 4.

22

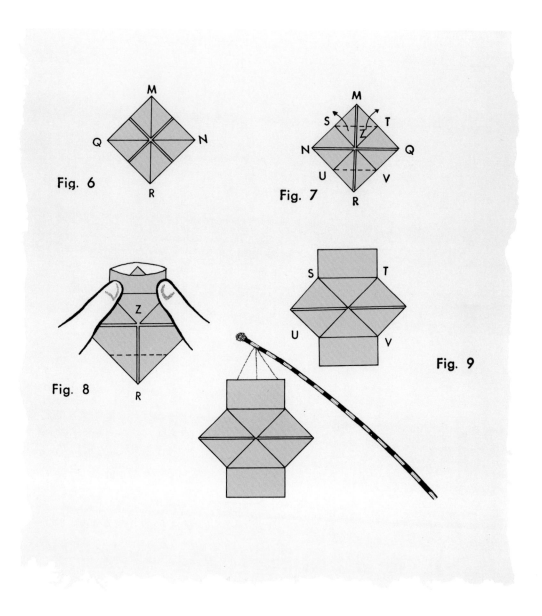

Fig. 6

Fig. 7

Fig. 8

Fig. 9

4. Turn the paper over once more and you will have Fig 5.
5. Next, fold the corners I, J, K and L forward once more to meet at the center. Turn the paper over and you will have Fig. 6.
6. Using both thumbs, push open MZ as in Figs. 7 & 8. Do the same with ZR and you will get Fig. 9.

fish

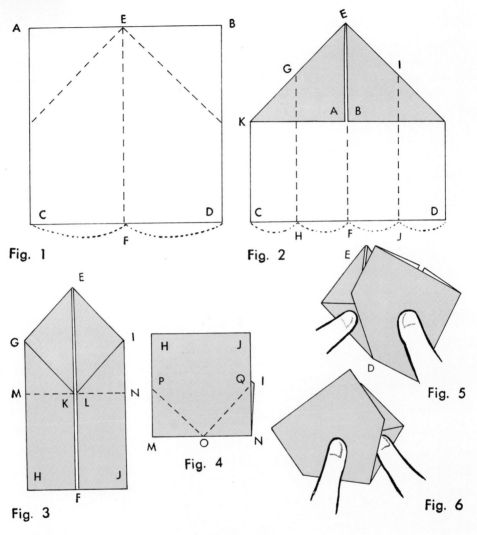

Fig. 1

Fig. 2

Fig. 3

Fig. 4

Fig. 5

Fig. 6

1. Fold a square piece of paper down the center at EF as shown in Fig. 1, crease, and then unfold.
2. Bring forward corners A and B until they meet along the center line EF, forming Fig. 2.
3. Fold at GH and IJ so that the edges KC and LD meet at the center line EF, as shown in Fig. 3.
4. Fold upward at MN so that HJ meets point E as in Fig. 4.

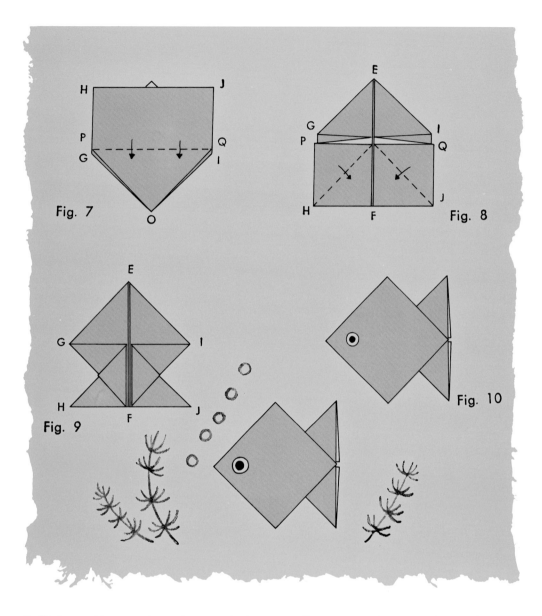

Fig. 7

Fig. 8

Fig. 9

Fig. 10

5. Pick up the paper and spread the two flaps HJ and GEI so that point M can be pushed up between them and extended as far as the center line EF. See Figs. 4, 5 & 6. Do the same with point N. The result will be Fig. 7.

6. Fold down the front flap at PQ in order to get Fig. 8.

7. Bend forward points P and Q so that they meet at F (Fig. 9).

8. Turn over and draw an eye as in Fig. 10.

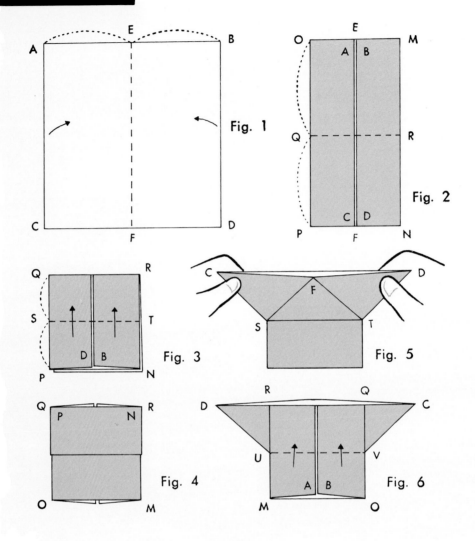

Fig. 1

Fig. 2

Fig. 3

Fig. 5

Fig. 4

Fig. 6

1. Take a square sheet of paper and fold it so that AC and BD (Fig. 1) meet at the center line EF and look like Fig. 2.
2. Fold OM back along the line QR so that OM meets PN. This will result in Fig. 3.
3. Fold along ST so that PN meets QR as in Fig. 4. Note that flap OM remains where it is for the present.

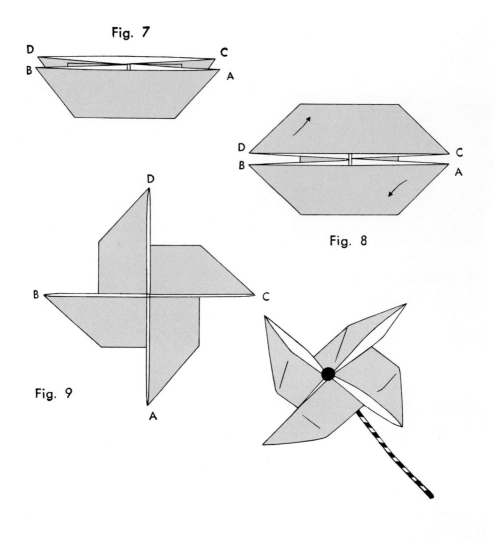

Fig. 7

Fig. 8

Fig. 9

4. Pull out corners D and C as in Fig. 5.
5. Turn the paper over and fold so that MO meets RQ (Fig. 6). Pull out corners A and B and you will get Fig. 7.
6. Spread out Fig. 7 so that it looks like Fig. 8.
7. Fold corner D upward and corner A downward and you will get Fig. 9.

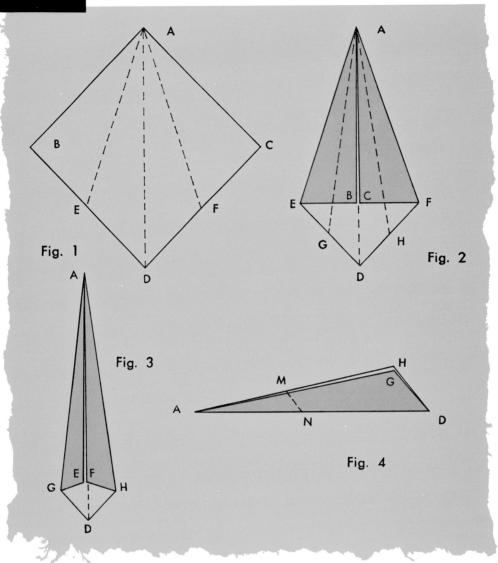

Fig. 1

Fig. 2

Fig. 3

Fig. 4

1. Crease a square piece of paper along line AD (Fig. 1) and then unfold.
2. Fold the edge AB forward to meet the center line AD. Do the same with the edge AC and you will have Fig. 2.
3. Now fold the edge AE forward so that it reaches the center line AD and then repeat with edge AF. You now have Fig. 3.
4. Fold along the center line AD so that AG is on top of AH as in Fig. 4.
5. To make the neck, pick up the paper with the open edge at the top and with corner A pointing to the left. Separate the two flaps slightly

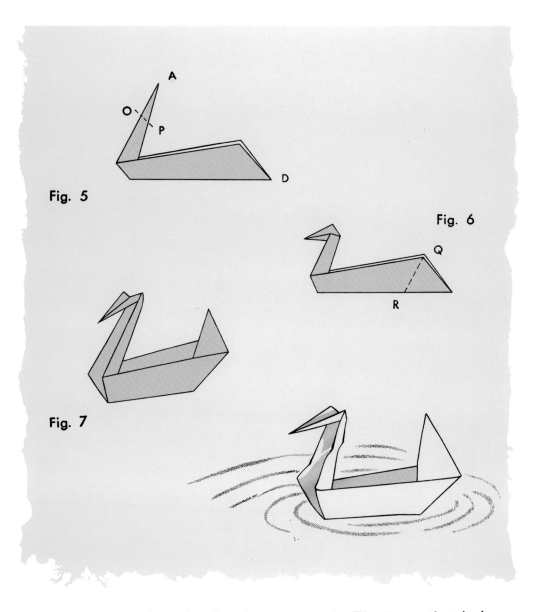

Fig. 5

Fig. 6

Fig. 7

and *b*end ba**ck** the pointed end at MN as in Fig. 5, so that it is **in**serted between the body flaps. In doing so, the fold along the line AD in the neck portion will be reversed.

6. The head is formed in a similar way at OP. See Fig. 6.

7. The tail is formed at QR (Figs. 6 & 7) in the same manner as the neck and head. Follow the diagrams carefully to get the proper angles for the neck, head and tail.

crane

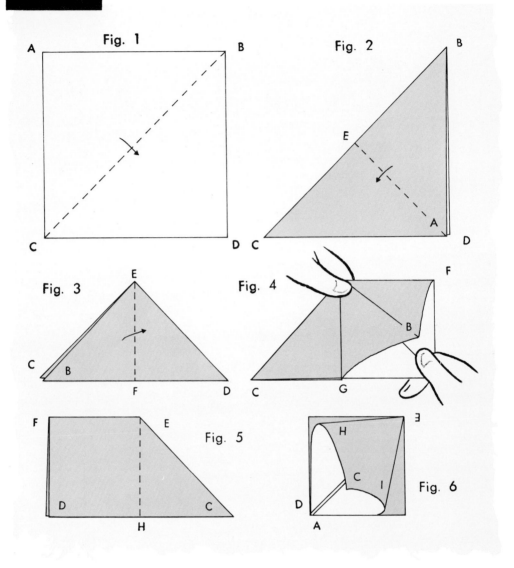

Fig. 1

Fig. 2

Fig. 3

Fig. 4

Fig. 5

Fig. 6

1. Fold a square piece of paper at BC (Fig. 1) so that point A is over point D as shown in Fig. 2.
2. Fold at ED so that point B is over point C resulting in Fig. 3.
3. As shown in Figs. 3 & 4, open B and bring it over until it is directly above D. Crease the paper along EF and EG.
4. Turn it over and you will have Fig. 5. Do the same with C as you did with B and the result will be Fig. 6.
5. Crease at YC and ZC (Fig. 7) so that points H and I meet along line EC, and then unfold.

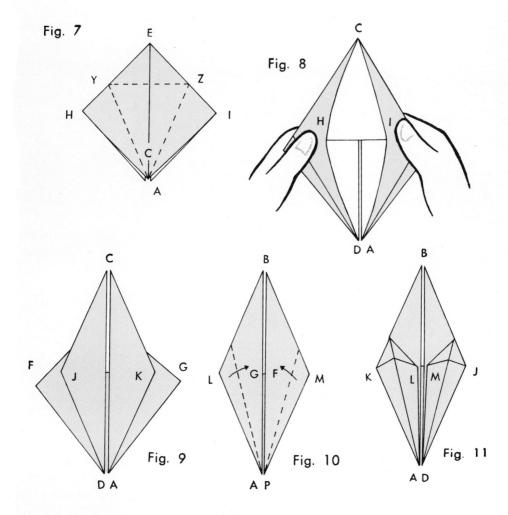

Fig. 7

Fig. 8

Fig. 9

Fig. 10

Fig. 11

6. Lift up C and fold at YZ so that H and I meet at the middle along line AC. Fig. 8 shows this step being executed and Fig. 9 shows it completed.

7. Turn the paper over and repeat steps 5 and 6. The result will be Fig. 10.

8. Fold on the dotted line shown in Fig. 10 so that L and M meet at the middle along lines BA and BD as shown in Fig. 11.

9. Turn the paper over and fold J and K the same way you did L and M. The result is shown in Fig. 12.

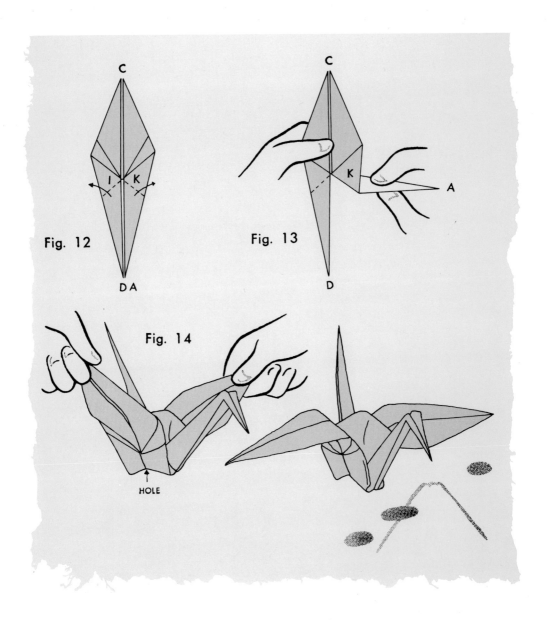

Fig. 12

Fig. 13

Fig. 14

HOLE

10. Lift A up toward the right as shown in Fig. 13 and fold at K. In doing so reverse the fold down the middle of this flap thus forming the neck.
11. Next make the head and then fold D to the left to make the tail. Head, neck and tail are made in the same way as those of the swan.
12. To complete, spread the wings (C and B) open and blow through the hole indicated in Fig. 14 in order to swell out the body.